Adrian Peterson

By Jeff Savage

AMAZING ATHLETES

Lerner Publications Company • Minneapolis

For Jack Sticha—future Vikings star

Lerner Publications Company
A division of Lerner Publishing Group, Inc.
241 First Avenue North
Minneapolis, MN 55401 U.S.A.

Website address: www.lernerbooks.com

Library of Congress Cataloging-in-Publication Data

Savage, Jeff, 1961–
   Adrian Peterson / by Jeff Savage.
       p.   cm. — (Amazing athletes)
   Includes bibliographical references and index.
   ISBN 978–0–7613–5746–9 (lib. bdg. : alk. paper)
   1. Peterson, Adrian—Juvenile literature. 2. Football players—United States—Biography—Juvenile literature. 3. Running backs (Football)—United States—Biography—Juvenile literature. 4. Minnesota Vikings (Football team)—Juvenile literature. I. Title.
GV939.P77S38 2011
796.332092—dc22 [B]   2010008049

Manufactured in the United States of America
1 – BP – 7/15/10

TABLE OF CONTENTS

A trainer cools off Minnesota Vikings' running back Adrian Peterson. The Vikings were playing against the Cleveland Browns in the first game of their 2009 season.

A PUNISHING FORCE

The Minnesota Vikings were playing the Cleveland Browns in their 2009 National Football League (NFL) season opener. But

Vikings' star **running back** Adrian Peterson was suffering from the heat and from running so hard. He sat in the visitors' locker room during halftime with a needle in one arm. The team doctor was pumping fluids through a tube into his body. The **trainer** was taping up a bloody gash on his other arm. Adrian had just thrown up.

At halftime, Adrian needed medical help to be able to play the rest of the game.

Adrian's team was trailing, 13–10. If he couldn't play in the second half, the Vikings would struggle to win.

After the second half **kickoff**, Adrian was back on the field. The Vikings drove to the one-yard

Adrian went back out on the field in the second half. He picked up yardage to help his team take the lead.

line. Adrian carried the ball into the **end zone** for a **touchdown**! The Vikings were ahead, 17–13.

After an **interception**, the Vikings had the ball again. Adrian pushed forward for gains of 6, 7, and 19 yards. The Browns struggled to stop him. With the Vikings at the Cleveland six-yard line, the focus was on Adrian. **Veteran quarterback** Brett Favre faked a handoff. Then he threw a pass to **wide receiver** Percy Harvin for an easy touchdown. The Vikings led, 24–13.

Brett Favre throws a pass to help the Vikings keep the lead.

Most of the fans at Browns Stadium had watched Adrian play on TV. They knew he ran with punishing force, making quick cuts. He'd lower his body to ram full speed into **defenders**. Cleveland fans were about to see Adrian at his best.

The Vikings were at the Browns' 36-yard line. The Vikings were already ahead by two scores. Adrian took his final handoff of the day. He slipped through two tackles and into the open field. He faked right and dashed left past **safety** Brodney Pool. At the sideline, Adrian made a sudden stop. He shoved **cornerback** Eric Wright out of bounds with his right hand. Adrian thundered down the sideline. Cornerback Brandon McDonald was the last to chase him. Adrian dumped him to the ground and ran for a 64-yard touchdown.

The Vikings won the game, 34–20. Favre was playing his first game with the Vikings. But he was in his 19th year as an NFL quarterback. After the game, Favre said, "I have never played with a running back like that."

On his last play in the game, Adrian dodged Browns defenders to run for a 64-yard touchdown.

The people of Palestine, Texas—Adrian's hometown—are proud of his skills and achievements.

ALL DAY

Adrian Lewis Peterson was born March 21, 1985, in Palestine, Texas. He lived with his family in a trailer on a dirt road. Adrian's family was athletic. His father, Nelson, played basketball at Idaho State University.

But his hopes of a career in basketball ended with a serious injury in a gun accident. During high school, Adrian's mother, Bonita, was a state champion sprinter. She later ran track at the University of Houston. Adrian's uncle Ivory Lee Brown was a running back for the NFL's Arizona Cardinals and Minnesota Vikings.

When Adrian was a toddler, his father gave him the nickname AD. The initials stood for All Day—as in running, jumping, and playing all day. "I never wanted to stop," said Adrian. "I never wanted to sleep. I just kept going all day."

Adrian loved football. His favorite team was the Dallas Cowboys. He was seven years old when he joined a peewee team. His father was his coach. Adrian was fast, so his father made him a running back.

Nelson Peterson *(left)* inspired Adrian to love sports, including football.

But Adrian wasn't as fast as his brother Brian, who was one year older. Adrian admired his big brother. He was a talented athlete and also got straight As in school.

One day in 1992, seven-year-old Adrian was playing football with friends. Brian was riding his bicycle nearby. Suddenly, a drunk driver crashed into Brian. "I was maybe 15 feet away," said Adrian. "I ran to him, screaming his name." Adrian held his brother and called his name. He got no response.

Brian's death crushed Adrian. He felt empty. He turned to football to forget his loss. To gain strength and speed, he made weights by filling old water jugs with sand. He tied the jugs to the ends of a pole and lifted them. He tied them to a rope and dragged them behind him in a sprint. He ran up and down a steep hill, frontward and backward.

In 1998, Adrian suffered another loss. His father was sent to prison for a drug-related crime. Adrian missed his father. He felt alone.

Adrian did not give up after losing his brother forever and his father to prison. "A lot of people make excuses when things happen in life. But I didn't want to go down that route. Instead of hanging my head, I make myself do better. I use it as motivation."

In 2000, Adrian's first year at Westwood High School, he suffered a knee injury. He missed the entire football season. He struggled in class. In 2001, he transferred to Palestine High School. Although he practiced with the football team, he wasn't allowed to play because of poor grades and because of the transfer. Adrian dreamed of being a professional football player. But he was running out of time. He focused in class and raised his grades. By the spring of 2002, he was allowed to play sports. He ran sprints on the track team and reached the state finals.

Adrian showed his blazing speed at running back as a junior at Palestine. In the team's second game, he rushed for 340 yards. He finished the 2002 season with 2,051 yards and 22 touchdowns. His senior year in 2003 was even better. He was fast enough to outrun defenders and strong enough to run them over. In one game, he flattened a **linebacker** and ran 88 yards for a score. In another, he scored six touchdowns in the first half. He averaged 11.7 yards per carry.

He ran for 2,960 yards and 32 touchdowns. By 2004, he was the top-rated running back in the nation.

Adrian shows off his game face in front of his locker at Palestine High. He was the top college pick among running backs in the country.

In 2004, as his mother looked on, Adrian signed a letter saying he would go to the University of Oklahoma. The boy in the back is one of Adrian's brothers.

BOOMER SOONER

Major college football programs throughout the country wanted Adrian. He visited colleges in California, Texas, Florida, and Oklahoma. Something at the University of Oklahoma caught Adrian's eye. Next to the Sooners' practice field, he saw players pulling heavily weighted sleds up a hill. "Man, this is intense," he thought to himself. "I knew that if I went [to Oklahoma], I wouldn't be cheating myself. I would definitely be getting some work done."

As a first-year Sooner, Adrian wasn't a starting player. But he gained over 100 yards in each of his first three games. Coaches made him a starter in the team's fourth game against Texas Tech. Adrian exploded for 146 yards and a touchdown. He remained a starter for the rest of the season. He broke the freshman college rushing record with 1,925 yards. He was second in the voting for the Heisman Trophy.

The Heisman award goes to college football's best player. The person is usually a junior or a senior, never a freshman.

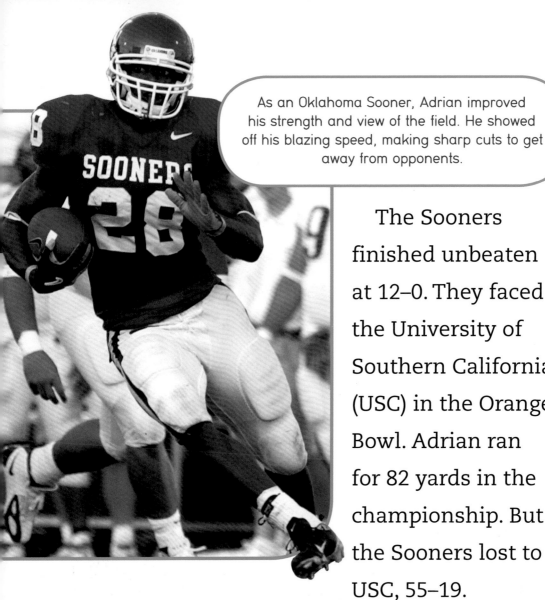

As an Oklahoma Sooner, Adrian improved his strength and view of the field. He showed off his blazing speed, making sharp cuts to get away from opponents.

The Sooners finished unbeaten at 12–0. They faced the University of Southern California (USC) in the Orange Bowl. Adrian ran for 82 yards in the championship. But the Sooners lost to USC, 55–19.

An ankle injury in 2005 caused him to miss time in four games. Still, he rushed for 1,108 yards and 14 touchdowns.

In 2006, during Adrian's junior year, his

father was let out of prison. Nelson got to see his son play in college for the first time against Iowa State. On one play, Adrian raced 53 yards. He dived into the end zone for a touchdown. Nelson celebrated with the rest of the crowd. Suddenly, the fans realized Adrian was hurt. He had a broken collarbone. Because of the injury, he missed the rest of the season. And NFL insiders wondered if he was prone to injuries.

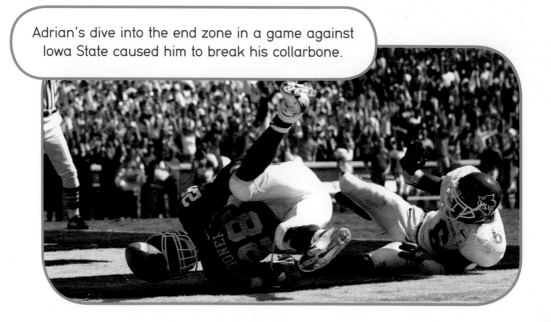

Adrian's dive into the end zone in a game against Iowa State caused him to break his collarbone.

At the 2007 NFL Combine, Adrian showed off his speed by running the 40-yard dash in 4.38 seconds.

ON THE ATTACK

In 2007, Adrian chose to skip his senior season. He felt he was ready to join the NFL. He took part in the NFL Combine. During this event, college players show NFL coaches their skills. The night before the combine, Adrian got a phone call in his hotel room. His half brother Chris Paris had been murdered. Adrian was stunned. His crying mother told him, "You've overcome a lot of obstacles. This is just another one." Adrian impressed coaches at the combine with his speed and power. Then he hurried home for Chris's funeral.

Adrian thought he was the best player in the 2007 NFL **Draft**. But the first six teams chose someone else. Experts thought maybe Adrian's injuries were the reason. The Minnesota Vikings picked Adrian with the seventh pick. "I'm blessed to be here with the Minnesota Vikings," said Adrian. "But to all the teams that passed on me, I'm like, no hard feelings, but you're gonna sit back one day and be like, 'Man, how did we let this kid go?'"

Surrounded by his family, Adrian displays a number 1 Vikings jersey. The Vikings had just chosen him as the seventh pick in the NFL Draft.

Adrian signed a six-year **contract** for over $40 million. He was rich. He wanted to prove he was worth the money. At training camp, he impressed coaches with his intensity. "I treat every practice as if it were a game," he said. "I've always had my mind set to be the best, and I know what it takes—hard work."

Adrian's first **regular season** NFL game was against the Atlanta Falcons. He rushed for 103 yards. He scored his first touchdown on a 60-yard pass reception. In week six, he ran for 224 yards against the Chicago Bears. This broke the Vikings team record for the most rushing yards in a game. Three weeks later, he broke the NFL record with 296 yards rushing against the San Diego Chargers. His jersey for that game was sent to the Pro Football Hall of Fame. One week later, he suffered a knee injury. He played hurt for the rest of the season. But he still finished with 1,341 yards. This was the second best in the NFL, after LaDainian Tomlinson.

Adrian scampers for yardage during a 2007 game against the San Diego Chargers. He ended the game with 296 yards—an NFL record.

Adrian was a rookie when he played in his first Pro Bowl. He ran for 129 yards and two touchdowns. He was named the game's Most Valuable Player.

Adrian was given several awards. He was named NFL Offensive **Rookie** of the Year. He was not satisfied. "We didn't make the **playoffs**," he said. "That's how it is with me. It's all about the team first."

In 2008, Adrian rushed for over 100 yards in five of the first eight games. He took the NFL lead in rushing and never let it go. He finished with 1,760 yards. But Adrian could not win by himself. As a team, the Vikings struggled to go far into the playoffs. The good news was help was on the way.

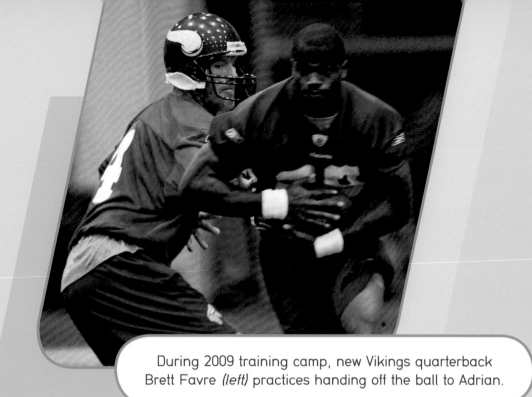

During 2009 training camp, new Vikings quarterback Brett Favre *(left)* practices handing off the ball to Adrian.

ALL BUILT UP

In 2009, the Vikings signed veteran quarterback Brett Favre. They also drafted rookie Percy Harvin to add speed at wide receiver. Adrian and Harvin often raced in practice to see who was the fastest. Coach Brad Childress said the offense would still focus on Adrian's running.

The plan worked. With Adrian running and Favre throwing, the Vikings roared to a 12–4 record. Adrian racked up eighteen rushing touchdowns—the most in the NFL.

Adrian had become the toughest running back in football. Adrian explained why he runs with such force. "I saw my brother get killed in front of me and [didn't have] my dad around when I was a kid. But I turned those things

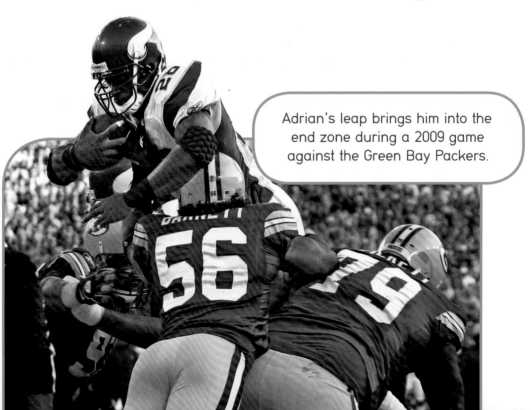

Adrian's leap brings him into the end zone during a 2009 game against the Green Bay Packers.

Head down, Adrian powers ahead for a touchdown during the NFC championship against the New Orleans Saints.

around and I use them as motivation. I run hard because it's all built up."

In the divisional playoffs, the Vikings crushed the Dallas Cowboys, 34–3. The Vikings were one win from the **Super Bowl**. But Minnesota's exciting season ended the following week. They played in the National Football Conference (NFC) championship against New Orleans. The Saints beat them in overtime, 31–28. The Saints went on to become Super Bowl champions.

Adrian prepares hard for games with intense strength training. Vikings strength coach Tom Kanavy says, "I've never had to speak to him about turning it up a notch. He attacks his workouts!"

Coach Childress admires Adrian's fierce desire in practice. But he says he has to keep Adrian under control too. "You have to slow him down and pull him by the belt loop and say, 'Whoa!'"

Adrian runs fast up and down hills. He reads his **playbook**. He tries to eat healthy foods. He does all he can think of to be the best. "I want to win Super Bowls, plural," Adrian says. "I want people to remember me as the best player to ever play this game. And not just the best at my position, but the best ever, period. When you think about football, I want my name to pop up in your head."

Selected Career Highlights

2009-2010
Named to the NFL All-Pro for the third time
Selected to the Pro Bowl for the third time
Ranked fifth in the NFL with 1,383 rushing yards

2008-2009
Named to the NFL All-Pro for the second time
Selected to the Pro Bowl for the second time
Ranked first in the NFL with 1,760 rushing yards

2007-2008
Broke the NFL all-time single-game rushing record with 296 yards
Ranked second in the NFL with 1,341 rushing yards
Named NFL Offensive Rookie of the Year
Named to the NFL All-Pro for the first time
Selected to the Pro Bowl and named Pro Bowl Most Valuable Player
Selected by Minnesota Vikings in the NFL Draft

2006-2007
Named first team All Big 12 Conference
Ranked third all-time at Oklahoma in rushing with 4,045 yards
Led Oklahoma with 1,012 rushing yards

2005-2006
Named first team All Big 12 Conference
Led Oklahoma with 1,108 rushing yards

2004-2005
Set NCAA freshman rushing record with 1,925 yards
Led NCAA in rushing attempts with 339
Finished second in the Heisman Trophy vote
Named first team All-America
Named first team All Big 12 Conference

2003
Named national high school Player of the Year
Set school records with 2,960 yards rushing and 32 touchdowns

2002
Rushed for school-best 2,051 yards and 22 touchdowns

Glossary

contract: a formal agreement signed by a team and a player

cornerback: a defensive player in midfield whose job is to stop running backs and wide receivers

defenders: players whose job is to stop the other team from scoring

draft: a yearly event in which professional teams in a sport take turns choosing new players from a selected group

end zone: the area beyond the goal line at each end of the field. A team scores a touchdown when it reaches the other team's end zone.

interception: a pass caught by a player on the defense. An interception results in the opposing team getting control of the ball.

kickoff: a kick of the ball that puts the football into play

linebacker: a defensive player who stands behind the front line of the defense

playbook: descriptions of a team's offensive and defensive plays

playoffs: a series of contests played after the regular season has ended

quarterback: a player whose main job is to throw passes

regular season: the regular schedule for a season. In the NFL, each team plays 16 games in the regular season.

rookie: a first-year player

running back: an offensive player whose main job is to run with the ball

safety: a defensive player whose main job is to stop passes to wide receivers

Super Bowl: the final game of each season between the champions of the American Football Conferences (AFC) and the National Football Conference (NFC). The winner of the Super Bowl is that season's NFL champion.

touchdown: a score in which the team with the ball gets into the other team's end zone

trainer: a person who teaches fitness through diet and exercise and helps players recover from injuries

veteran: a player with years of experience

wide receiver: a player who catches passes, mainly for big gains

Further Reading & Websites

Currie, Stephen. *Adrian Peterson*. Broomall, PA: Mason Crest Publishers, 2009.

Kennedy, Mike, and Mark Stewart. *Touchdown: The Power and Precision of Football's Perfect Play*. Minneapolis: Millbrook Press, 2010.

Sandler, Michael. *Adrian Peterson*. New York: Bearport Publishing, 2010.

Savage, Jeff. *Brett Favre*. Minneapolis: Lerner Publications Company, 2011.

Adrian Peterson Fan Site
http://www.adrianpeterson.com
A website for Adrian Peterson fans features a biography, photos, statistics, and a video of some of Adrian's greatest plays.

Minnesota Vikings: The Official Site
http://www.vikings.com
The official website of the Minnesota Vikings includes the team's schedule and game results, late-breaking news, biographies of Adrian Peterson and other players and coaches, and much more.

Sports Illustrated Kids
http://www.sikids.com
The *Sports Illustrated Kids* website covers all sports, including football.

Index

Photo Acknowledgments

Photographs are used with the permission of: AP Photo/Tony Dejak, p. 4; AP Photo/Paul Jasienski, pp. 5, 7; © Dilip Vishwanat/Getty Images, p. 6; AP Photo/Mark Duncan, p. 9; © Aaron M. Sprecher/The New York Times/Redux, p. 10; © Michael Downes/The New York Times/Redux, p. 12; AP Photo/Tyler Morning Telegraph, Tom Worner, p. 15; AP Photo/Tyler Morning Telegraph, David Branch, p. 16; AP Photo/Jerry Laizure, p. 18; © Matthew Emmons/US Presswire, p. 19; AP Photo/Michael Conroy, p. 20; © Sporting News/ZUMA Press/Icon SMI, p. 22; AP Photo/Tom Olmscheid, p. 23; AP Photo/Hannah Foslien, p. 25; AP Photo/Mike Roemer, p. 26; © Ronald Martinez/Getty Images, p. 27; AP Photo/Paul Spinelli, p. 29.

Front cover: © Scott Boehm/Getty Images.